ANIMALS IN HIDING

Michael Salaka

HABA®

PowerKiDS press™

NEW YORK

Published in 2018 by The Rosen Publishing Group, Inc.
29 East 21st Street, New York, NY 10010

First Edition

Editor: Melissa Raé Shofner
Book Design: Michael Flynn

Photo Credits: Cover JMx Images/Shutterstock.com; p. 5 Fabio Maffei/Shutterstock.com; p. 6 Take Photo/ Shutterstock.com; pp. 9, 24 (fur) John McMahon/Shutterstock.com; pp. 10, 24 (wings) Gianna Stadelmyer/ Shutterstock.com; p. 13 YoONSpY/Shutterstock.com; p. 14 Nantawudth Ngoenjan/Shutterstock.com; p. 17 Foto Mous/ Shutterstock.com; p. 18 swapan banik/Shutterstock.com; p. 21 Christian Musat/Shutterstock.com; p. 21 (inset) Stan Osolinski/Getty Images; pp. 22, 24 (spots) elleon/Shutterstock.com.

Cataloging-in-Publication Data

Names: Salaka, Michael.
Title: Animals in hiding / Michael Salaka.
Description: New York : PowerKids Press, 2018. | Series: Animals in my world | Includes index.
Identifiers: ISBN 9781538321485 (pbk.) | ISBN 9781538321508 (library bound) | ISBN 9781538321492 (6 pack)
Subjects: LCSH: Camouflage (Biology)–Juvenile literature. | Animals–Juvenile literature.
Classification: LCC QL751.5 S25 2018 | DDC 591.47′2–dc23

Manufactured in the United States of America

CPSIA Compliance Information: Batch #BS17PK: For Further Information contact Rosen Publishing, New York, New York at 1-800-237-9932

Please visit: www.rosenpublishing.com and www.habausa.com

CONTENTS

In the Trees

Many animals live in the jungle. They can be hard to see. They're very good at hiding. Can you find the frog? It looks just like a leaf!

Snakes can be many colors. This snake is bright green. It hides in a tree. The snake's head looks like a leaf. This helps the snake hide.

Sloths live in trees. They have long, brown fur. Their fur looks like a tree. Sloths move very slowly. Plants grow on them. This makes sloths hard to see.

On the Plants

Butterflies have pretty wings. They can be many colors. Some have spots that look like eyes. This butterfly has red wings. It's hard to see on a red flower.

Caterpillars are very small. They live on plants. This caterpillar is green. It has brown parts, too. It looks like a leaf. This helps the caterpillar hide.

In the Water

Crocodiles have dark skin. They love to swim. Crocodiles swim under the water. Their skin looks like a log or a rock. This makes crocodiles hard to see.

Hippos live in rivers and lakes. They walk underwater. Only their face can be seen. Hippos eat plants in the water. Sometimes these plants help them hide.

On the Ground

Tigers have orange and white fur. They have black stripes, too. Tigers like to hide in the grass. Their stripes make them hard to see.

Tapirs are black and white. They're also very big. Baby tapirs have spots and stripes. It makes them look like sticks and rocks. This helps baby tapirs hide.

Jaguars have orange fur. They have lots of black spots. Jaguars like to hide in grass. They like to hide in trees, too. Their spots make them hard to see.

WORDS TO KNOW

fur

spots

wings

INDEX